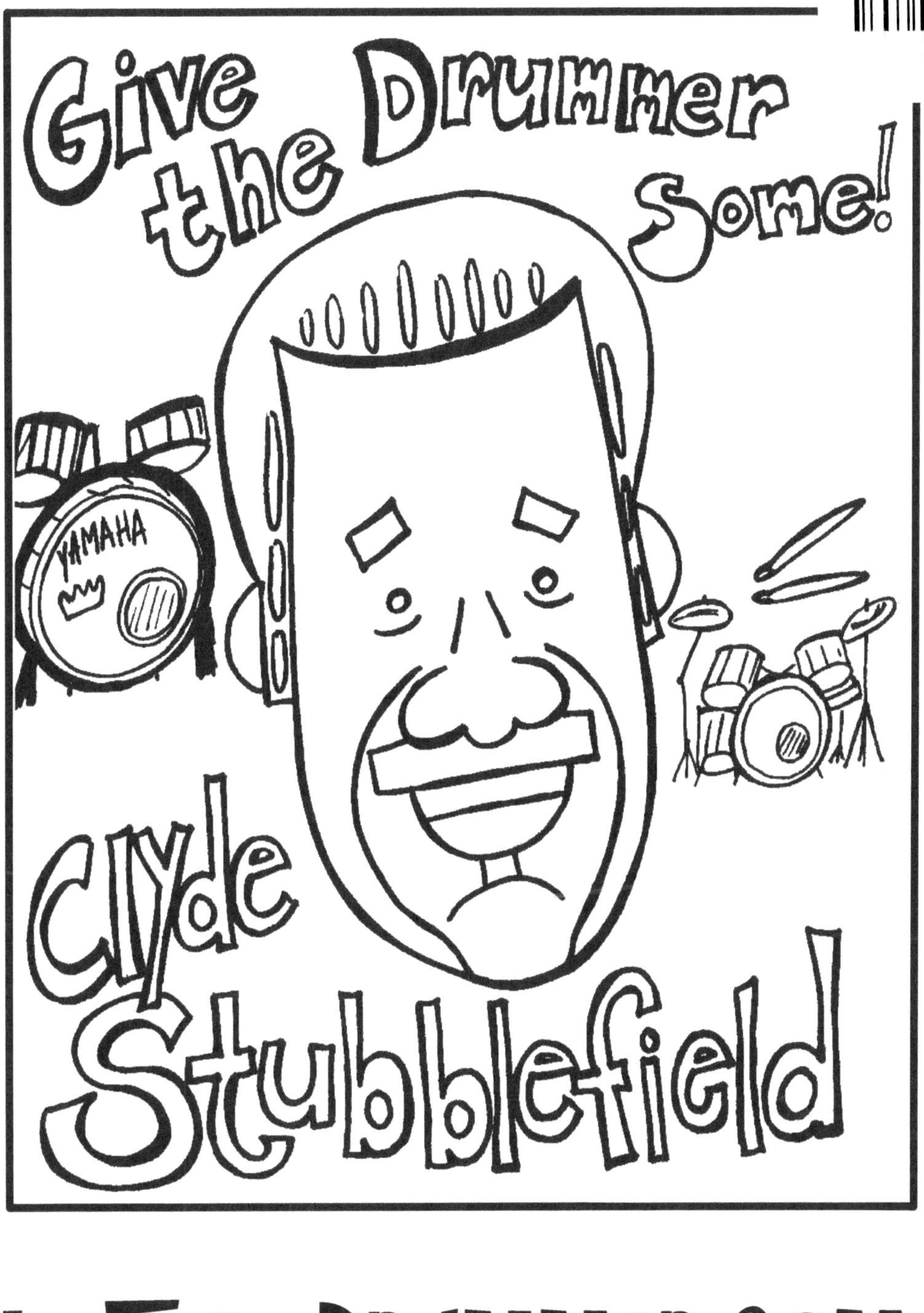

Give The Drummer Some!
A Clyde Stubblefield Coloring Book

By Carolynn Schwartz aka Soulmama

ISBN-13: 978-1546449478
ISBN-10: 1546449477

DEDICATION

To Clyde Stubblefield who will continue to inspire generations of drummers to get those booties shakin!

THANK YOU

To Joey Banks, Violet Moran, Rick Tvedt, Tommy Strader, and everyone involved in The Clyde Stubblefield Scholarship Fund and The Coalition to Recognize Clyde Stubblefield, for ensuring that Clyde's legacy will remain intact and that young musicians in Madison who want to learn to play will always have that opportunity.

ABOUT THE AUTHOR

Carolynn Schwartz is many things: a wife and mother of two boys, a singer/songwriter, Southern Wisconsin's SoulMama, a podcaster, a voice actor, an activist, a crafter, a blogger, and a doodler. She learned to doodle from her mother, but took it to the next level when she discovered the meditative nature of coloring with her own children. Each word is lovingly drawn freehand with a sharpie, a vague plan, and a sense of whimsy.

The images in this book were all drawn in the days and weeks after Clyde Stubblefield's death on February 18, 2017. Carolynn got her nickname SoulMama, from Clyde himself and introduced her on stage as such every Funky Monday. She performed with him in the Funky Monday band and The Clyde Stubblefield All-Stars at The King Club, The High Noon Saloon, and at countless festivals, weddings, and parties over the course of a decade. She also played a few games of poker with him and a table full of drummers now and then.

Also created and drawn by Carolynn Schwartz:
"We will not be silent: Signs form the Women's March
"PANTSUIT NATION: The Coloring Book"- inspired by the FB group and HRC
"Interesting Insults & Other Creative Curses to Color" - super sweary
"Interesting Insults & Other Creative Curses to Color: Volume 2"
"Interesting Insults & Other Creative Curses to Color: Volume 3, The Abecedarium"
"I Adulted Today and other Delightful Doodles" – this is a *clean* book

She also collaborated with NYC blues singer and life coach Dave Rudbarg to create
 "I am allowed to be human, and other affirmations from Coach me Dave,"
- a positive book to color while contemplating your course in life.

These books are all available at **www.createspace.com**

These books and other wonderful things like greeting cards, totes bags, stickers and individual downloadable coloring pages are also available at her Etsy Shop: SoulMama's Stuff
https://www.etsy.com/shop/SoulMamasStuff

Please check out her various endeavors by visiting the following websites:

https://www.facebook.com/soulmamasstuff
https://www.soulmamasays.wordpress.com
https://soundcloud.com/carolynn-schwartz-black (music and voice-over stuff)
http://www.cdbaby.com/cd/carolynnblack (let it go)
http://www.cdbaby.com/cd/carolynnblack2 (livin in a ball factory)
https://www.facebook.com/TheSchwartzes (duo with her Hubby)
https://soundcloud.com/user-948975692 (The Schwartzes SoundCloud Page)

About Clyde Stubblefield

Also known as **The Original Funky Drummer**, Clyde Stubblefield had the dubious honor of being the most sampled drummer in the known universe. He is most famous for a 20 second drum pattern he played during the James Brown song "The Funky Drummer" - 20 seconds that changed the sound of r&b forever and arguably launched rap and hip-hop into existence.

Born in Chattanooga, TN, Clyde had with no formal musical training. He listened to the marching bands that would parade through town, and to the trains clickety-clacking and echoing off the hillsides and developed his own style and the now famous "ghost beat." By 1965 he was playing with the JBs and over the years recorded a string of hits with including "Cold Sweat," "I got the feelin," and "Say it loud - I'm black and I'm proud." He was one of two drummers who played with Mr. Brown during that time, sharing the stage with John "Jabo" Starks who became a lifelong friend and fellow "Funkmaster."

In 1971, Clyde left James Brown's band and moved to Madison , WI where his brother Frank was living. After playing with a number of bands he created The Clyde Stubblefield Band and established **Funky Monday**, a tradition that would continue off and on for 40 years and still does even after his death. While he would occasionally take trips to NY or LA to play with his fellow James Brown alumni, he always called Madison home and was often heard saying "I LOVE YA MADISON" from behind the drumkit.

I had the great honor to meet Clyde when my hubby and I were visiting Madison in 2004. We had just bought a house here and would be moving from NYC in a few months. We walked into The King Club on a Funky Monday in May, and long story short, I ended up on stage that night singing with The Funky Drummer! Not long after I was in the band and one night he introduced me as "Southern Wisconsin's SoulMama!" Well, when Clyde gives you a nickname, you KEEP it! I sang with him and The Funky Monday Band and then The Clyde Stubblefield All-Stars off and on over the years, sometimes so pregnant that all I could do was waddle in front of his drum kit, sometimes while holding one of my kiddos, and sometimes with my husband. Playing with him was one of the great joys of my life. He was possibly the most generous musician to work with, always giving people the opportunity to shine and encouraging young musicians to get on stage. To think of all the young drummers who have had the chance to play on his kit is heartwarming. I will miss him, his smile, and his spirit immensely, for a long time to come. I will NOT miss his ability to take all my money at the poker table!

In 2015, **The Coalition to Recognize Clyde Stubblefield** created **The Clyde Stubblefield Scholarship Fund,** which has now partnered with **The Madison Area Music Awards (MAMAs),** in an effort to get Clyde the recognition we all know he deserves AND get instruments in kids' hands AND help them get to music school. All of the Funky Monday shows since then have been fundraisers for the scholarship fund.

On Feb 18, 2017, Clyde died after a long battle with renal disease. He was 73. **The University of Wisconsin** is giving Clyde a **Ph.D in Drumming**, posthumously this May and the All-Stars will be playing at the Memorial Union Terrace in celebration of his life and musical legacy. Joey B Banks, the force behind The Clyde Stubblefield All-Stars, was a student of Clyde's and has long been a champion of music for the youth of our community, and continues to lead the band as he pays tribute to his musical hero each time he steps behind the kit. He produced a live cd from a show we had at The Barrymore theater in 2015 that you can buy at our monthly Funky Monday shows at The High Noon Saloon in Madison, WI.

So why a Clyde Stubblefield Coloring Book? My first reason is a selfish one. I love to draw and in times of stress it actually helps me to cope. In the days and weeks after his death I was so sad, understandably so, but I knew I had to keep my chin up somehow and get on with the daily business of life with two children and a husband. So I thought of Clyde and the things he would say, and I could hear him and see his smile, and soon I was drawing and feeling better. One page turned into another and before long I realized I was creating a new book. Secondly, I'd like to help raise money for the Scholarship Fund. I know what the power of music can do and how amazing it is to give a child an instrument or send them to music school, so I will donate a portion of the proceeds of the sale of this book indefinitely. And thirdly, who doesn't like to color? Put on a copy of "Revenge of The Funky Drummer" or "The Original" and get out your markers or pencils and get groovy! These drawings are meant to be fun and remind you of being at a Funky Monday show. Four of the images are actually the lyrics to the one song Clyde wrote "Party's in the Kitchen" while others are things he said or songs he played on. There is even a page highlighting a mere 70 of the hundreds of artists who have sampled that 20 second drumbeat. I bet you'll be singing along as you color before you know it.

If you would like to donate to The Clyde Stubblefield Scholarship Fund go to clydescholarship@paypal.com.

If you want to know where to see The Clyde Stubblefield All-Stars, go to https://www.facebook.com/clydestubblefieldallstars/

Table of Funky Contents

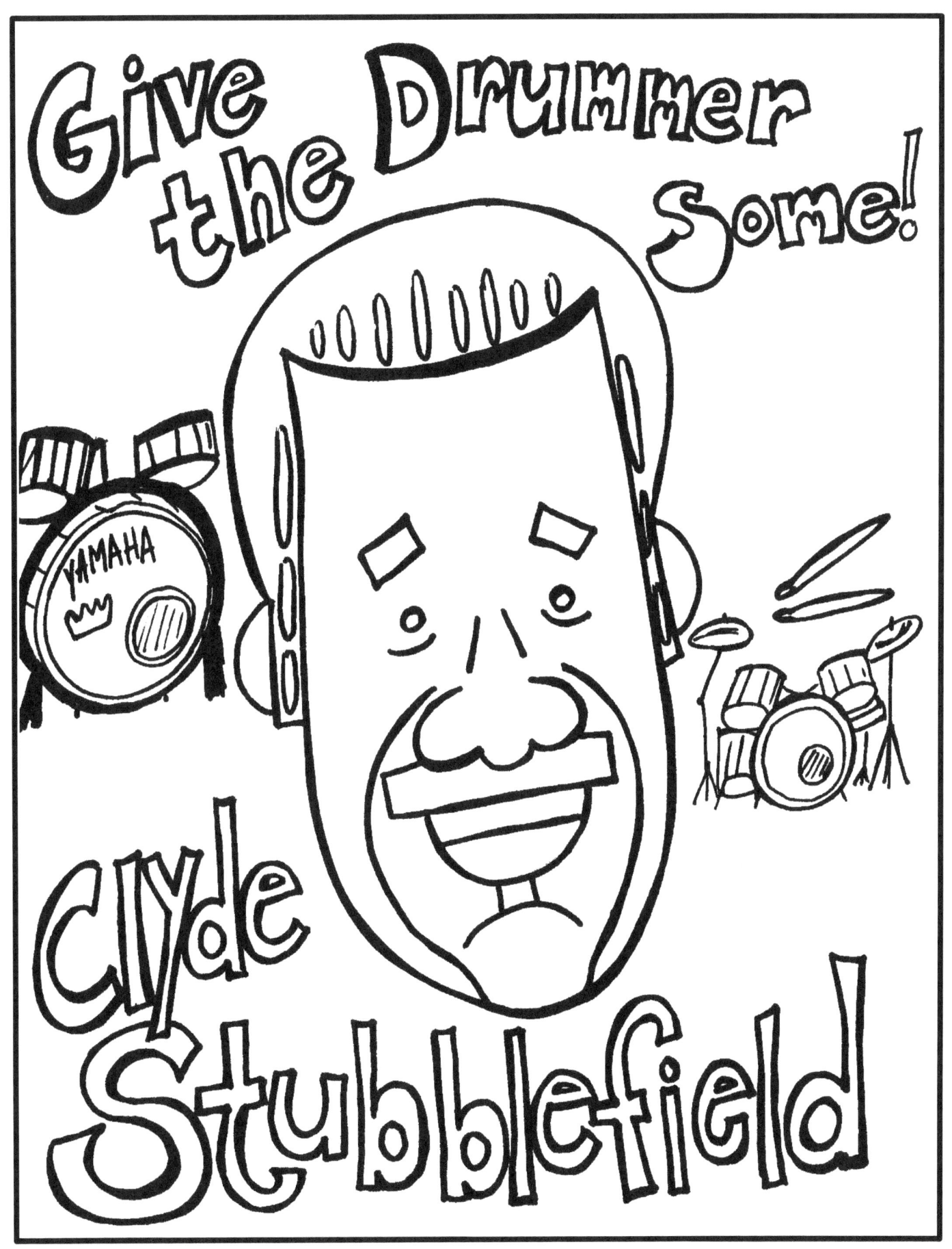

CHATTANOOGA

Clyde

Austin

Stubblefield

MADISON

4/18/1943-
2/18/2017

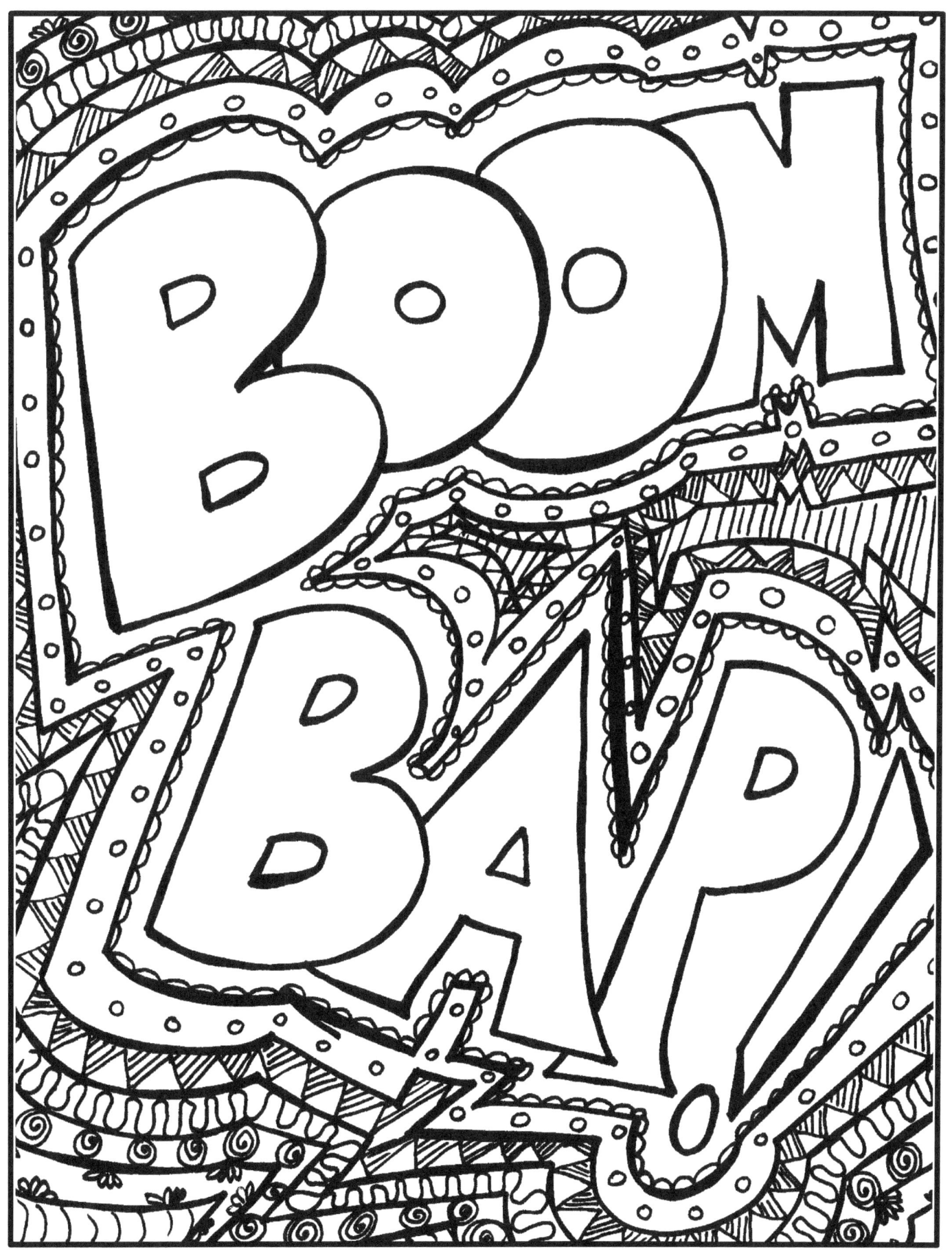

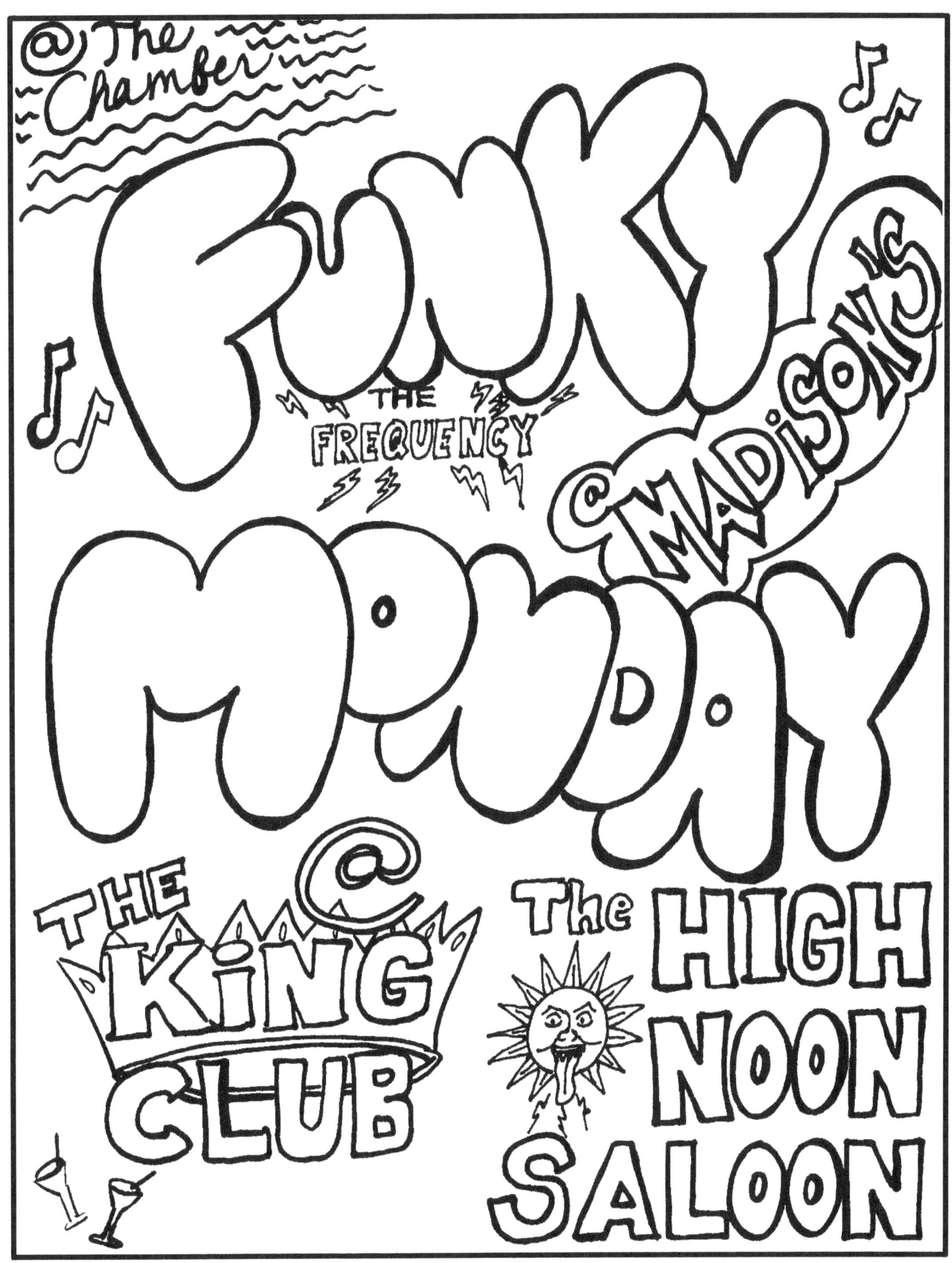

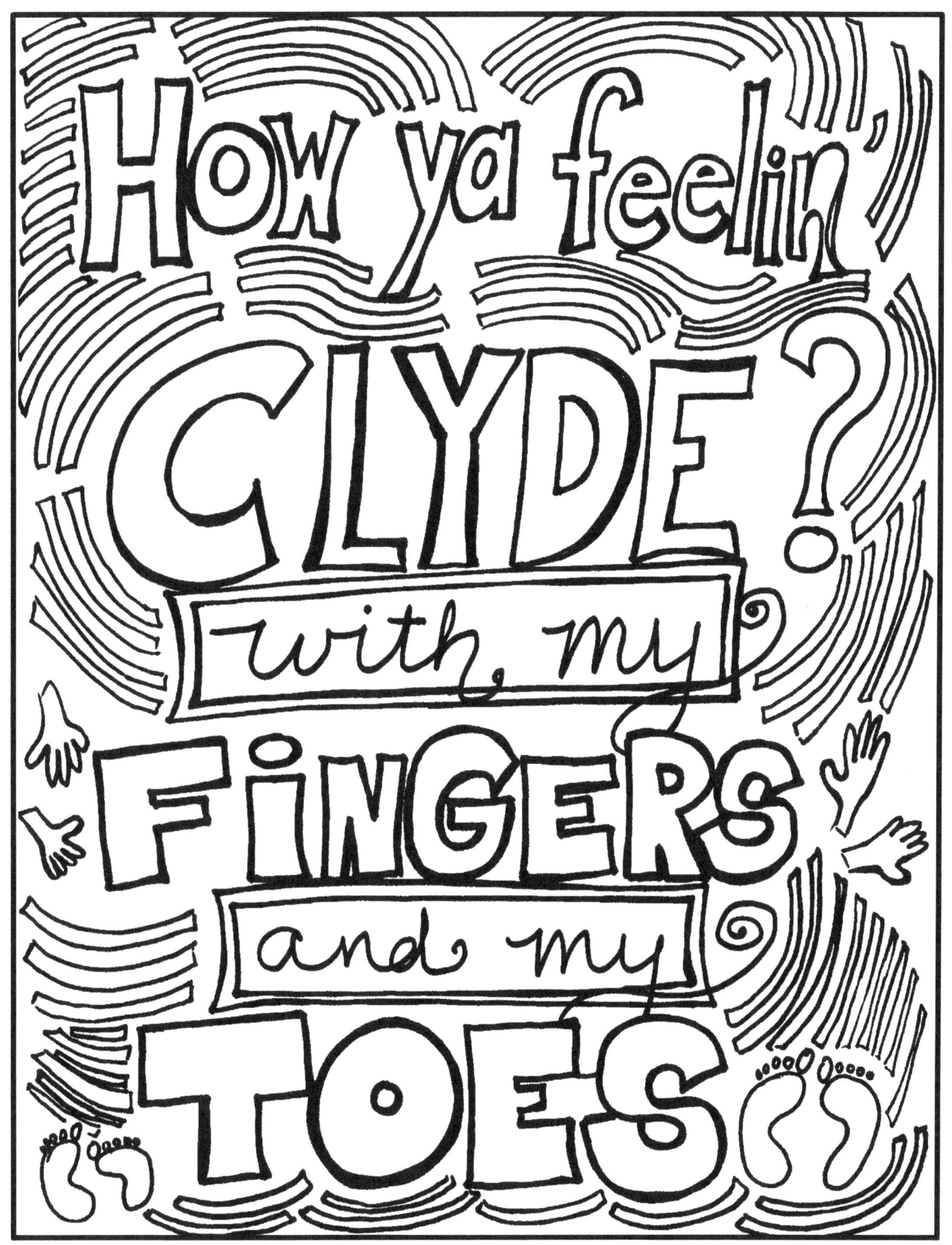

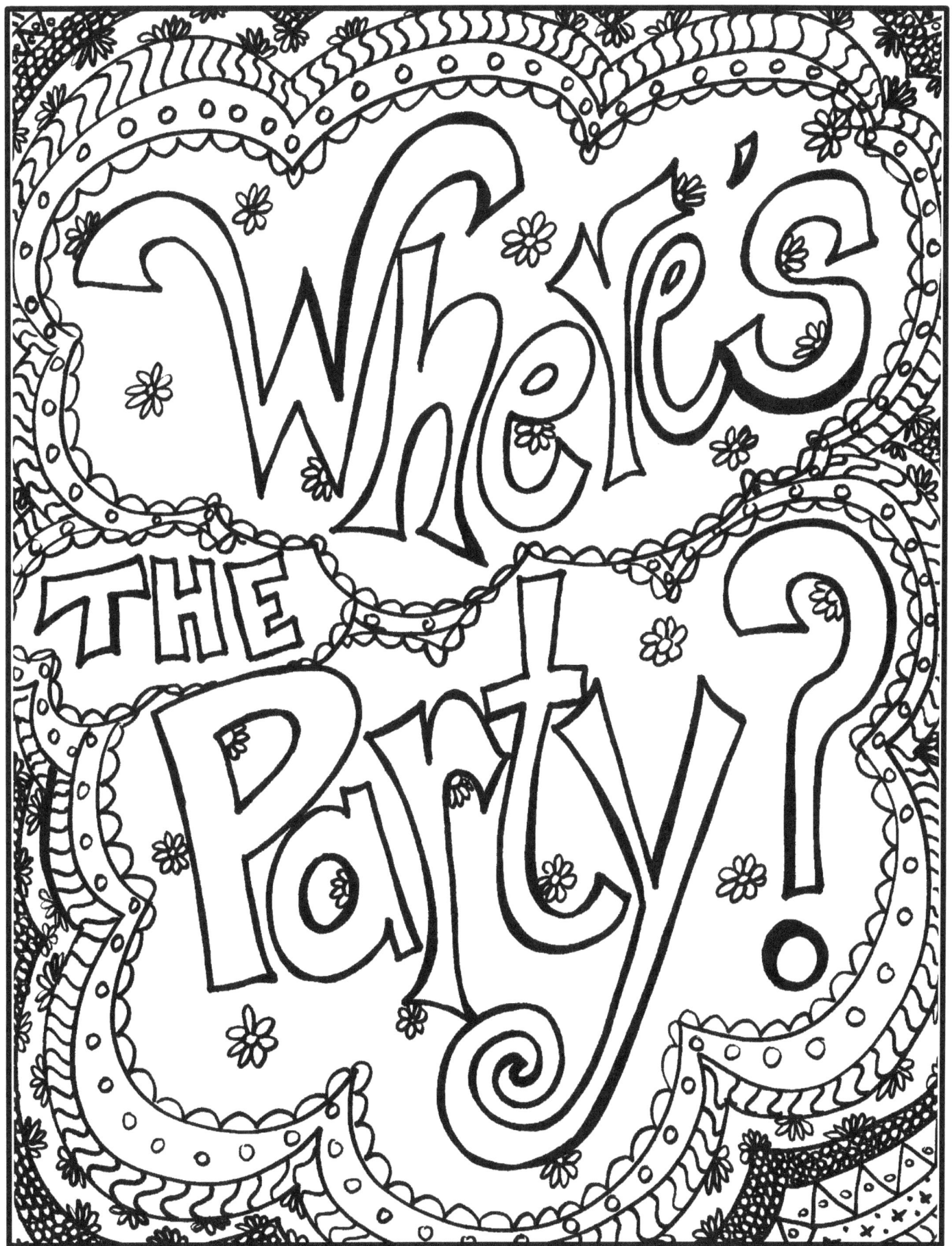

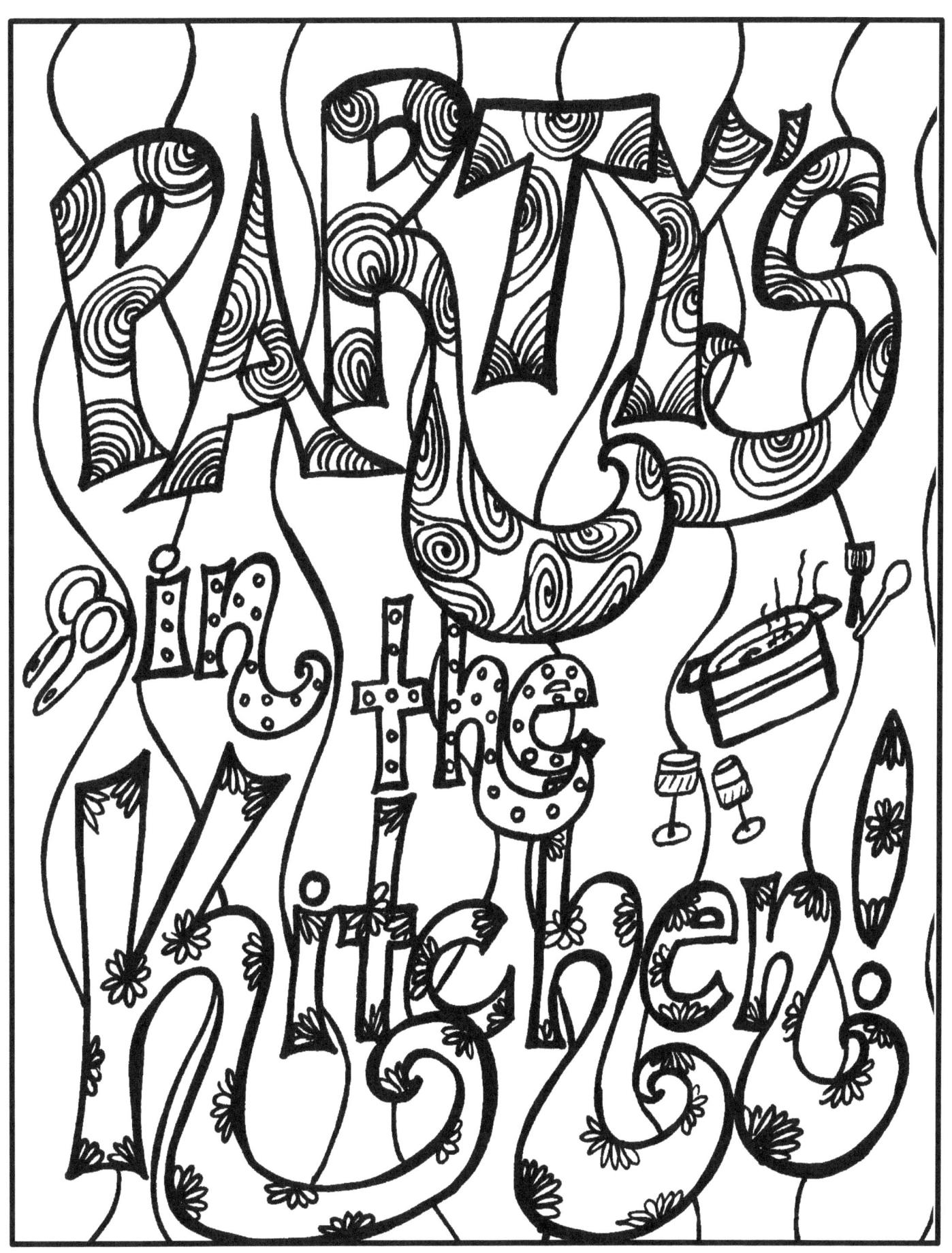

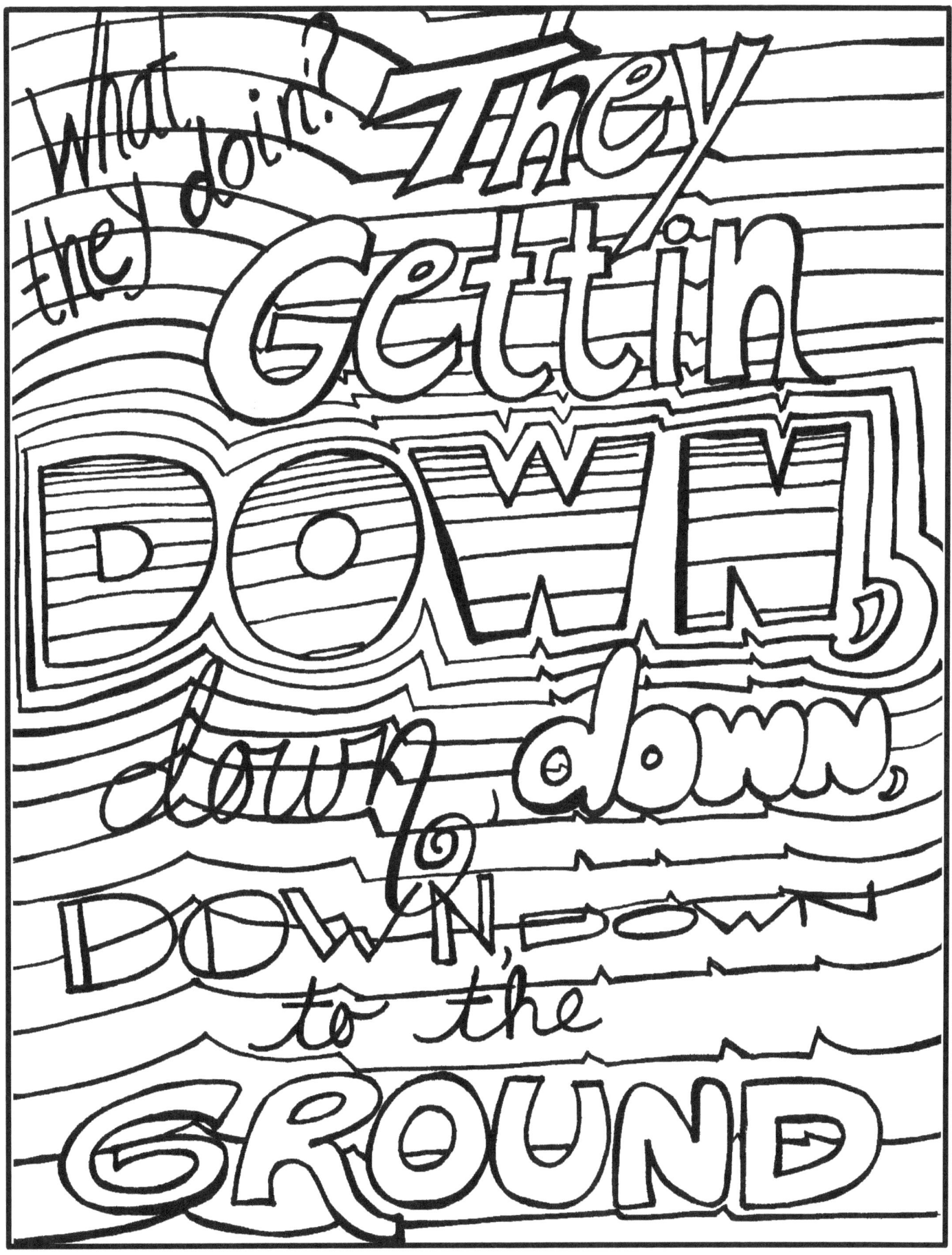

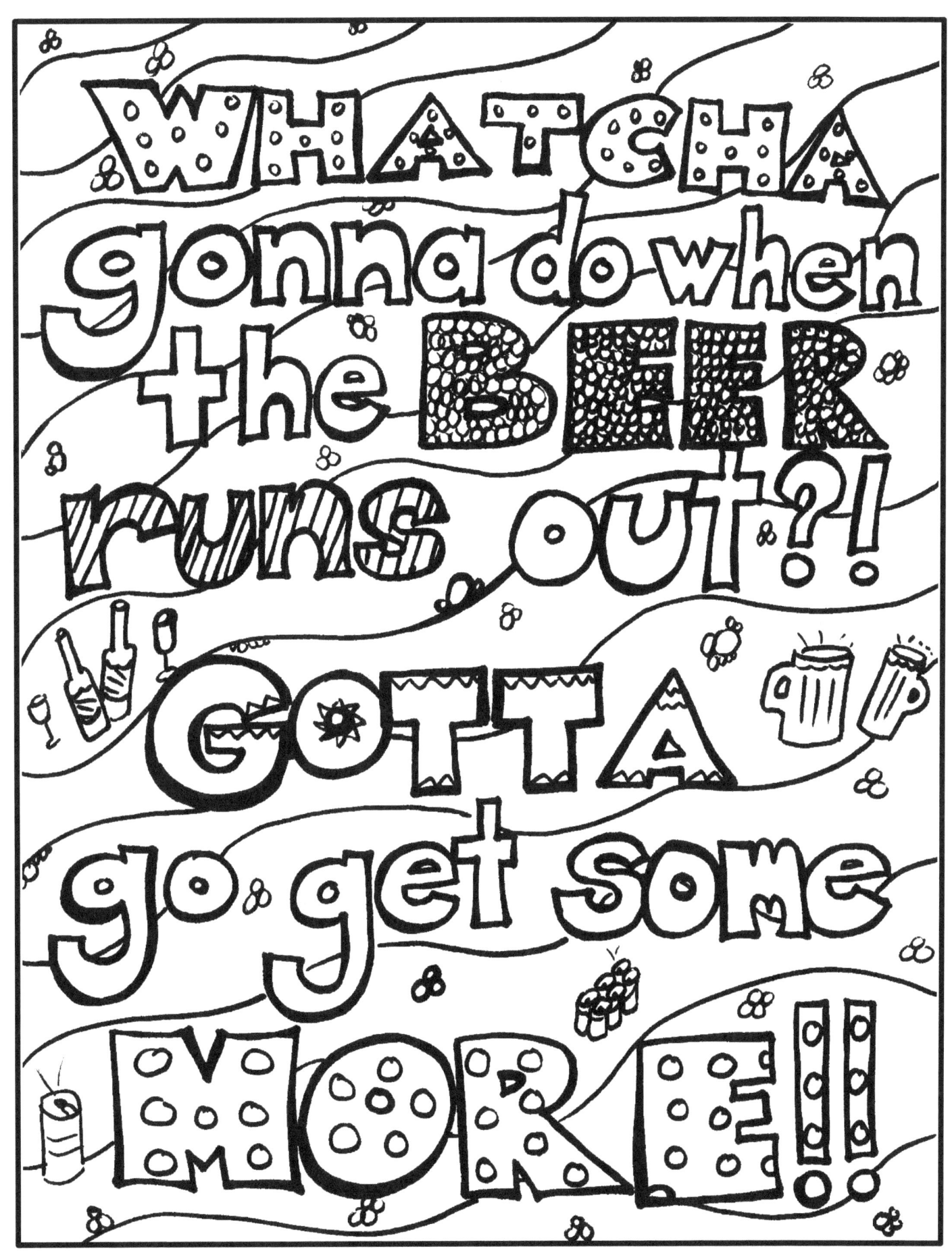

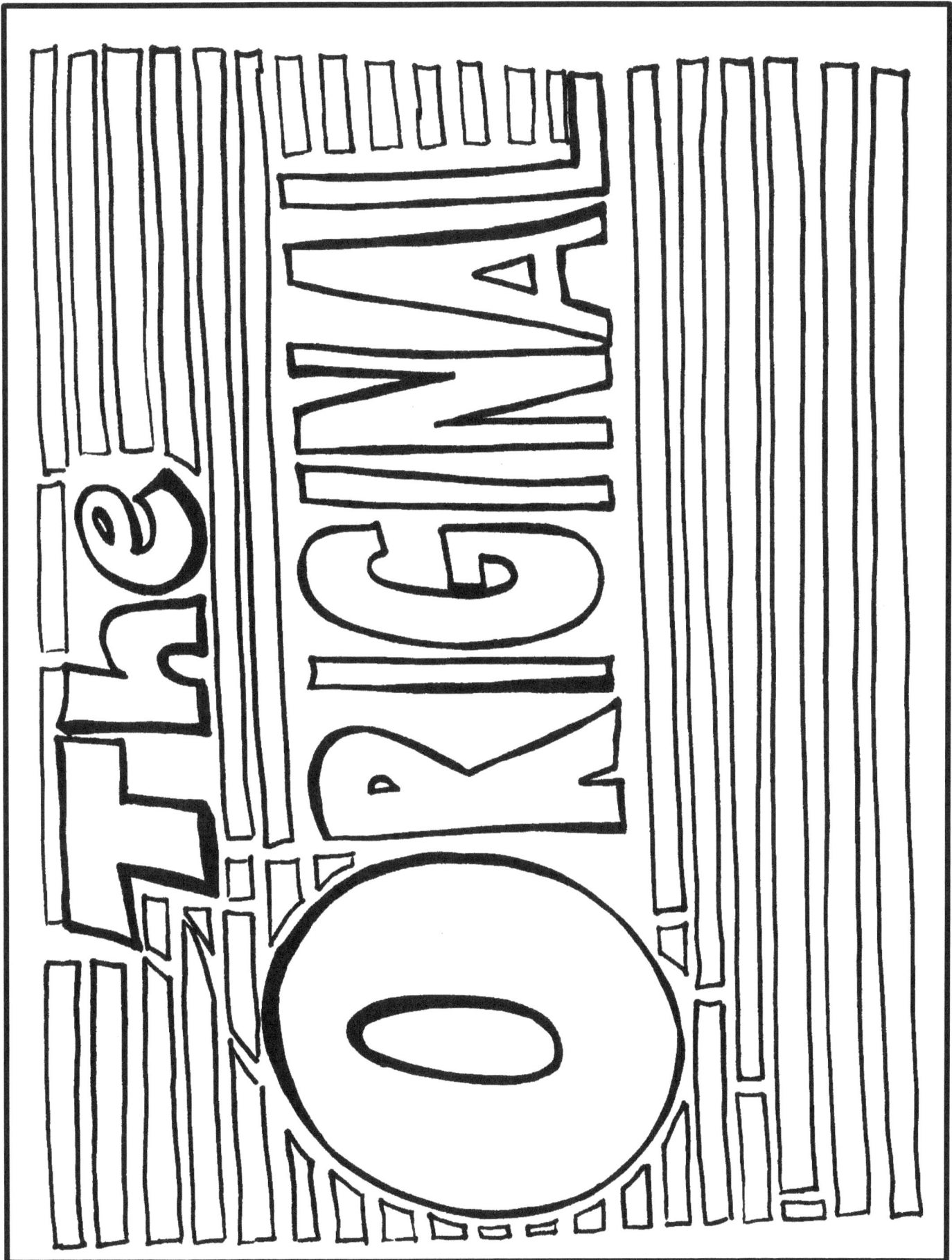

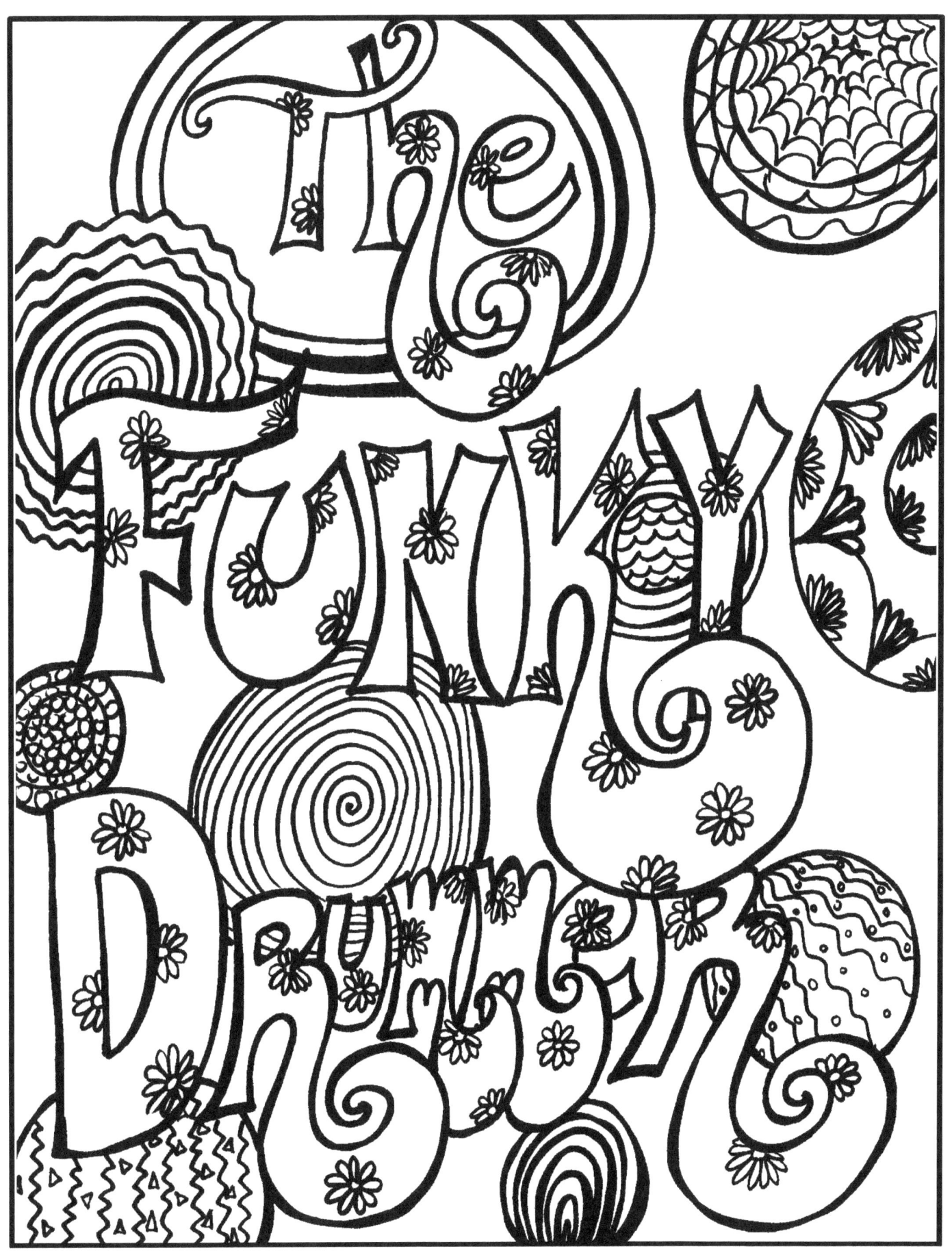

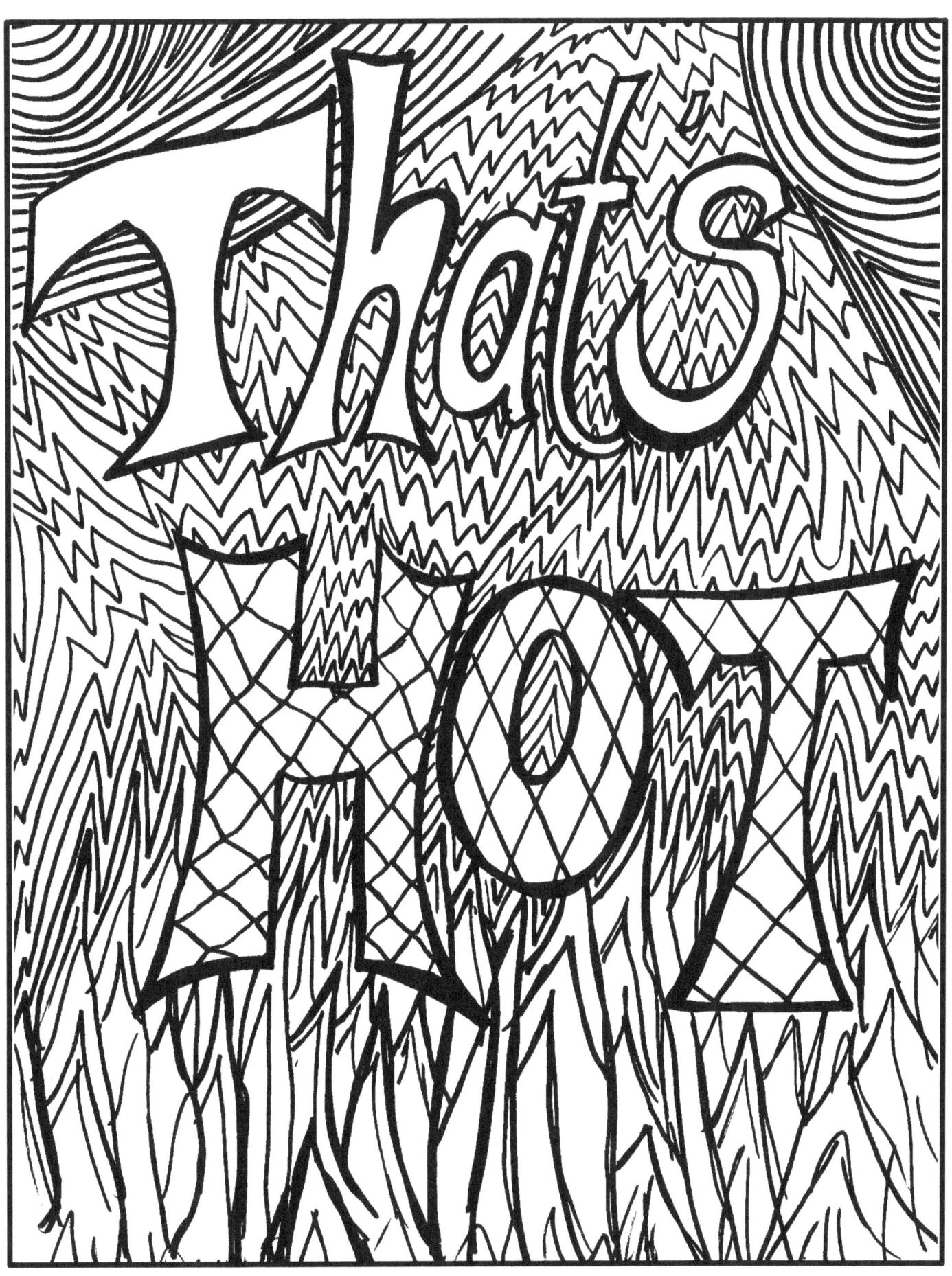

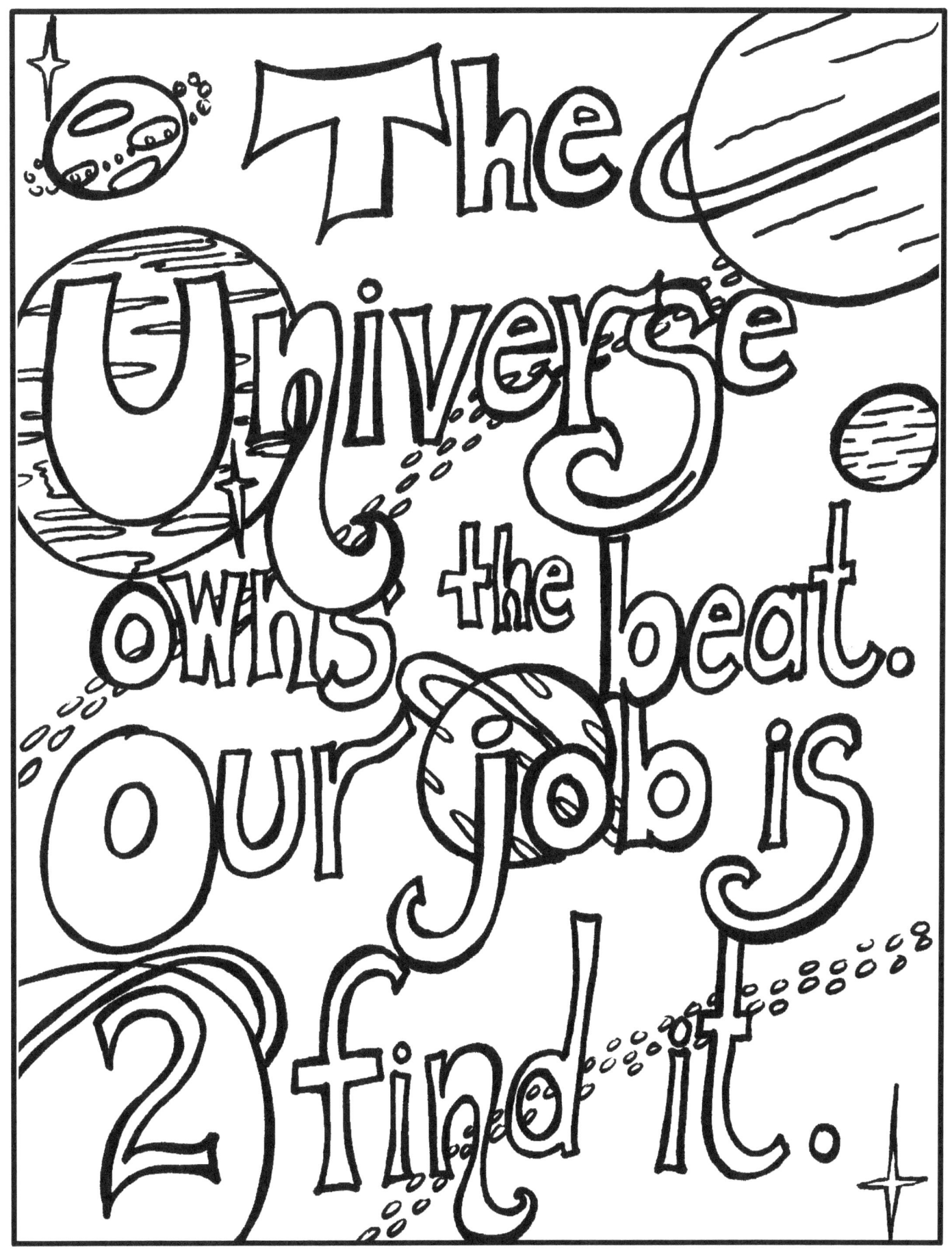

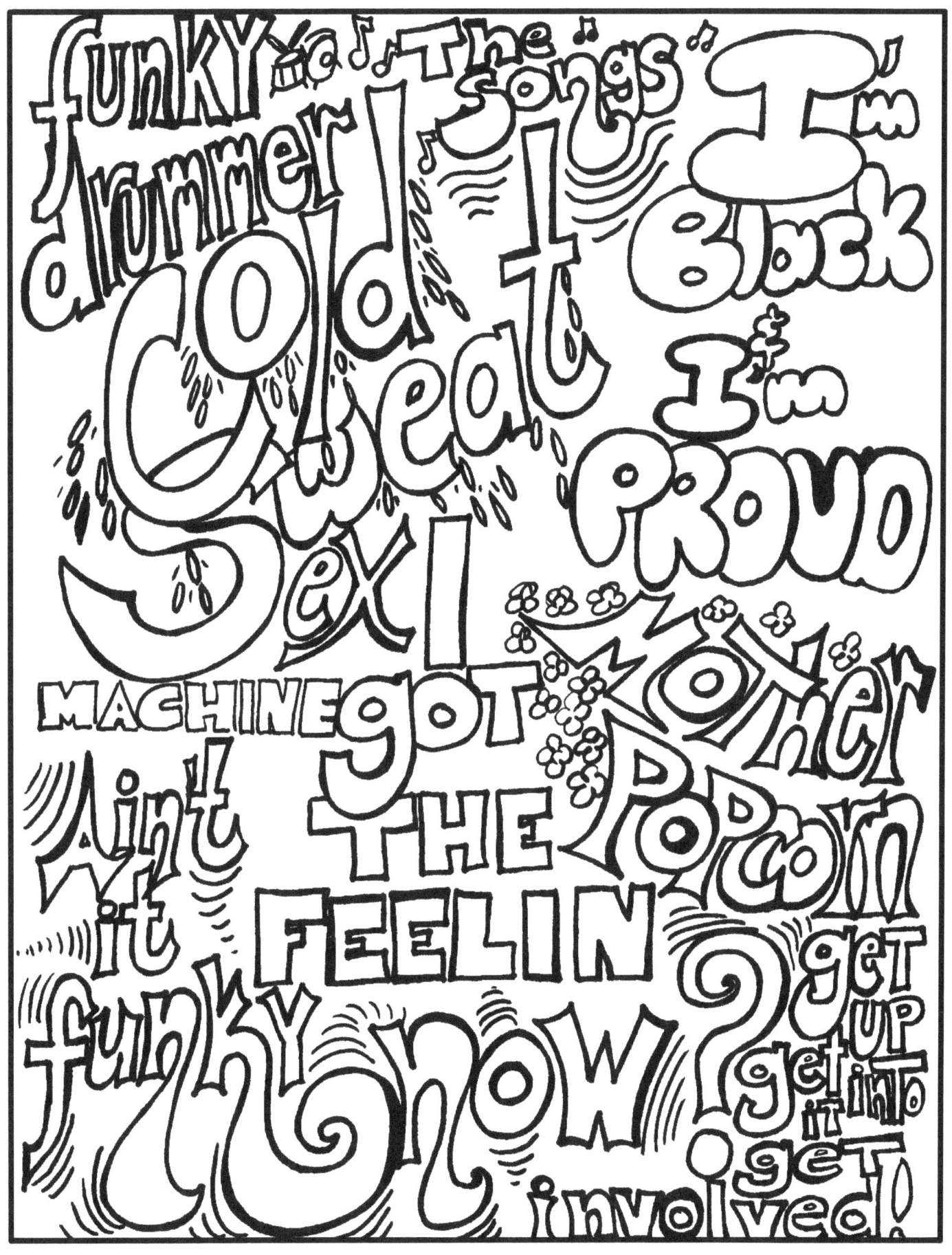

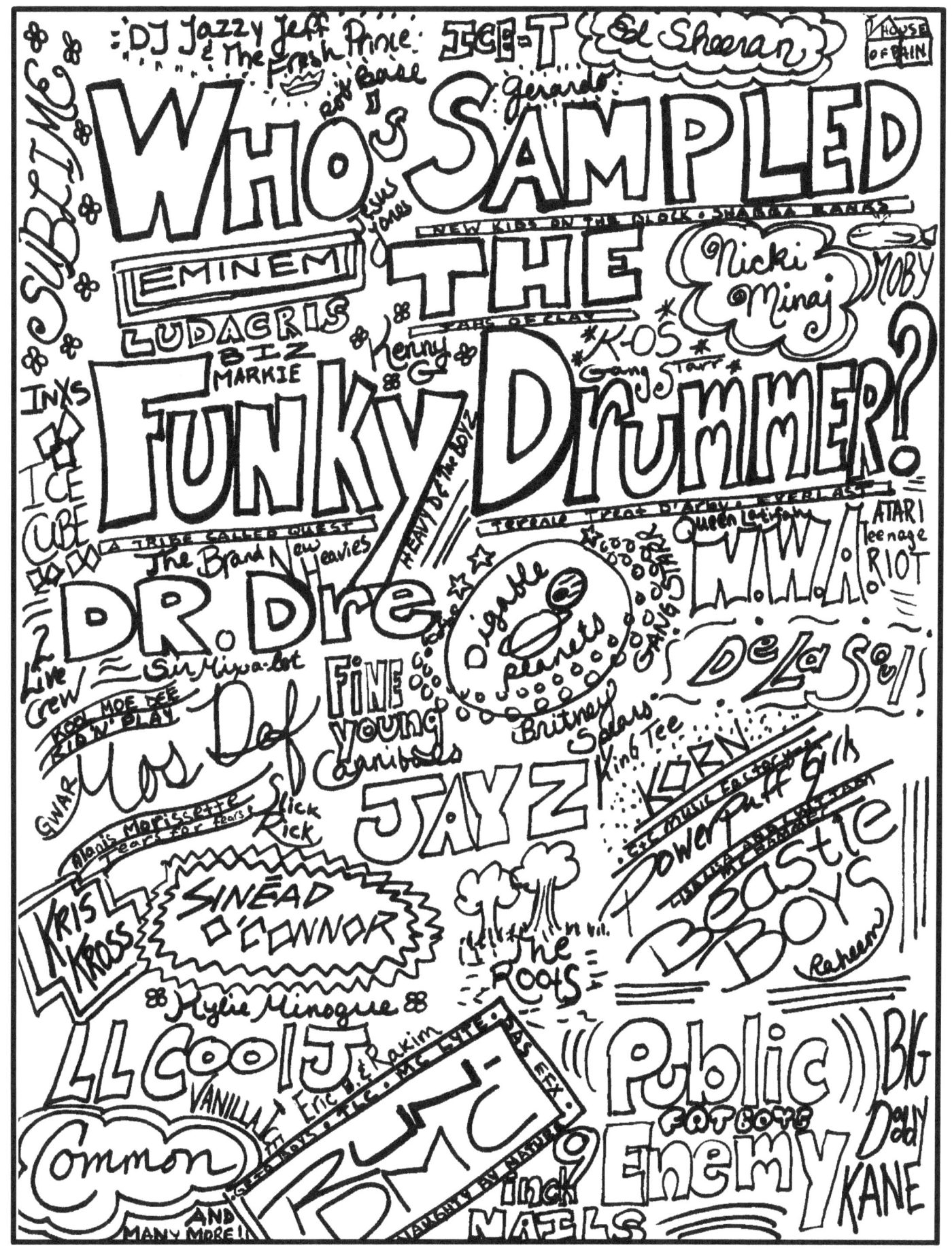

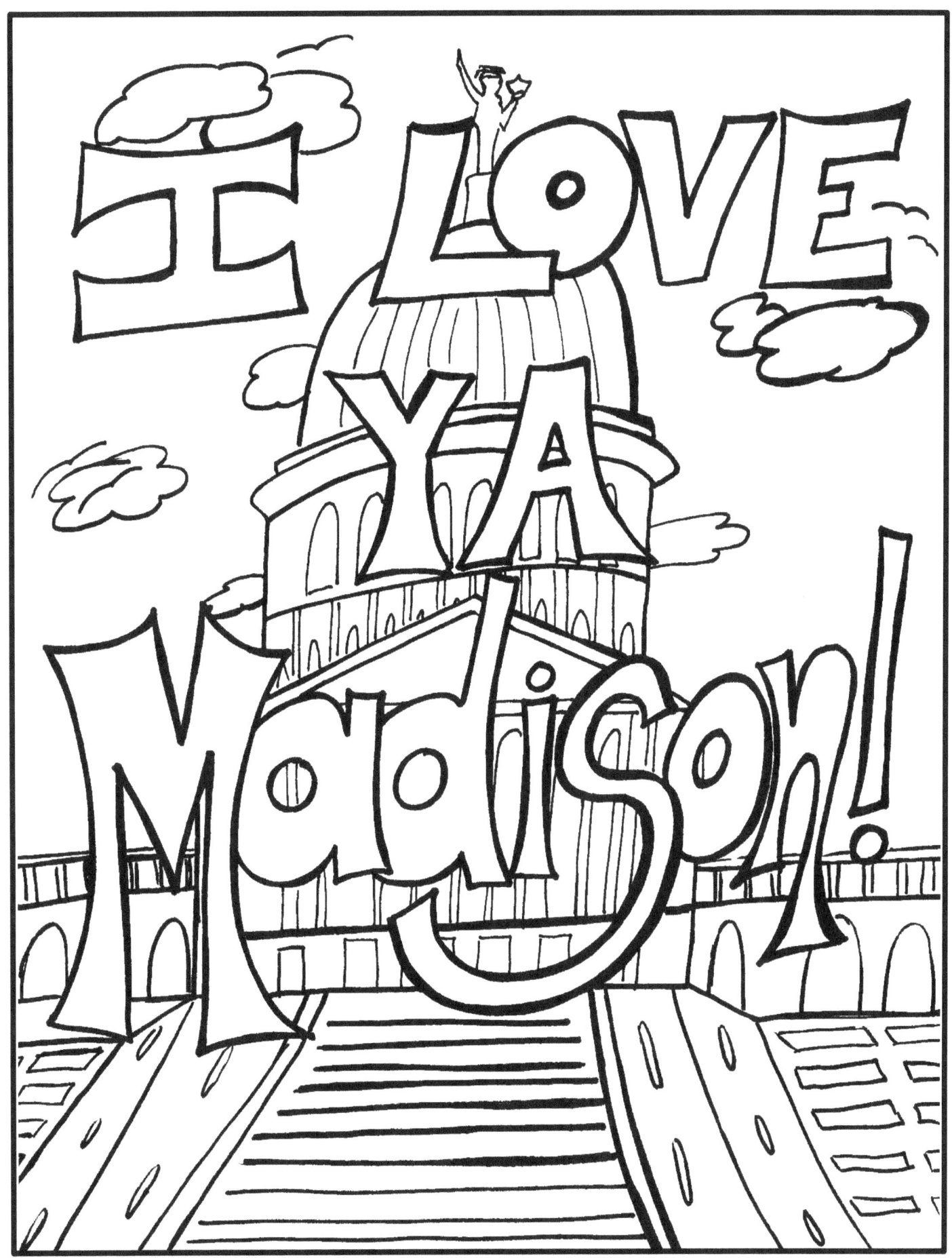

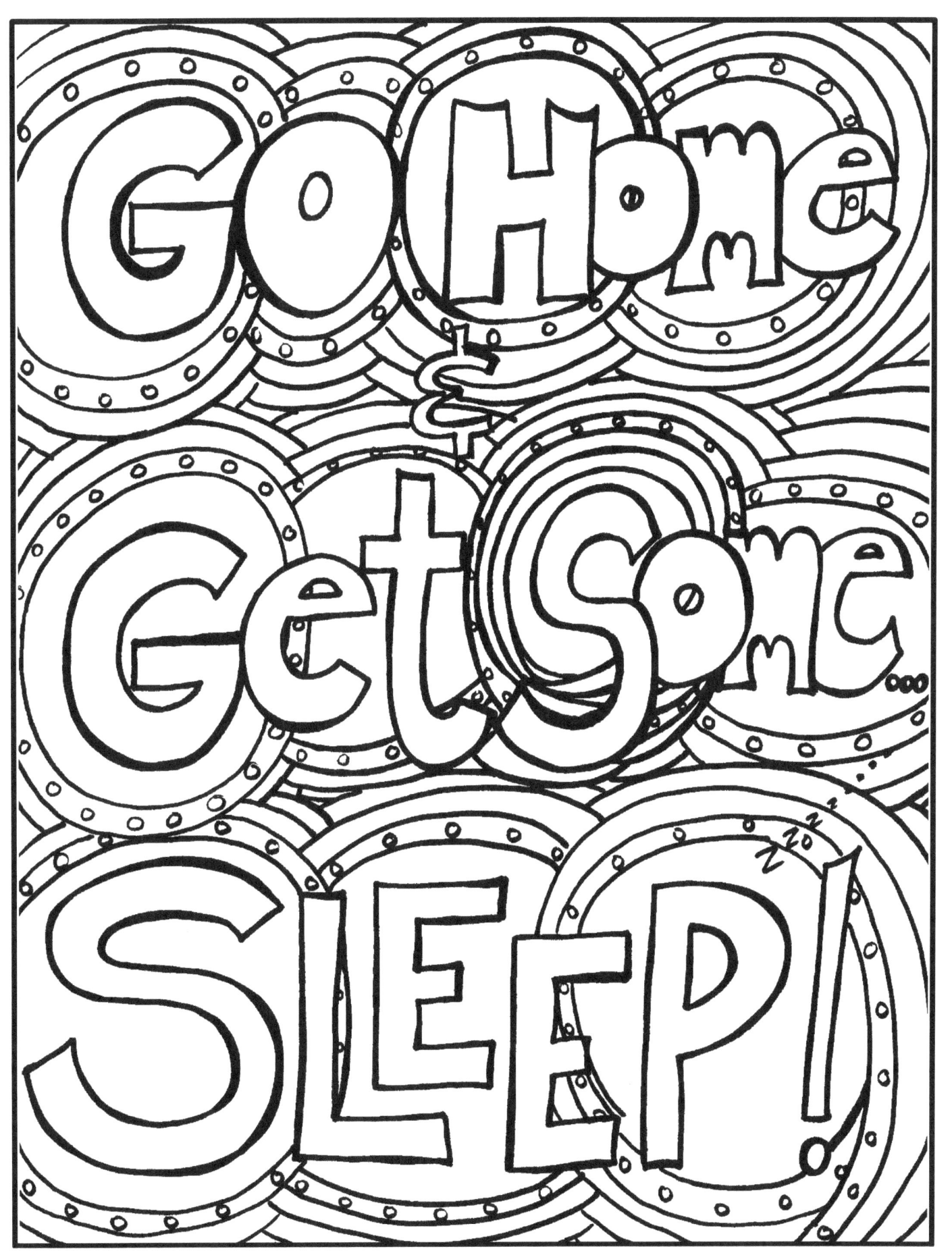

ISBN-13: 978-1546449478
ISBN-10: 1546449477